NATIONAL
GEOGRAPHIC

T0045532

The Shopping List

Sue Whiting

Tony helps his dad at
the supermarket.
Tony gets a shopping basket
for all the things they need.

The shopping list shows what
Tony and his dad need to buy.

Shopping List
bananas
sausages
buns
ice cream
toothbrushes
dog biscuits

Where are the bananas?

The bananas are with the fruits and vegetables.

Shopping List

~~bananas~~

sausages

buns

ice cream

toothbrushes

dog biscuits

Where are the sausages?

The sausages are with the meat.

Shopping List
~~bananas~~
~~sausages~~
buns
ice cream
toothbrushes
dog biscuits

Where are the buns?

The buns are with the bread.

Shopping List
~~bananas~~
~~sausages~~
~~buns~~
ice cream
toothbrushes
dog biscuits

Where is the ice cream?

The ice cream is with
the frozen foods.

Shopping List

~~bananas~~

~~sausages~~

~~buns~~

~~ice cream~~

toothbrushes

dog biscuits

Where are the toothbrushes?

The toothbrushes are with the toothpaste and soaps.

Shopping List
- ~~bananas~~
- ~~sausages~~
- ~~buns~~
- ~~ice cream~~
- ~~toothbrushes~~
- dog biscuits

Where are the dog biscuits?

The dog biscuits are with the
pet food.

Do Tony and his dad have
everything on the list?

Yes, Tony and his dad have everything on the list!

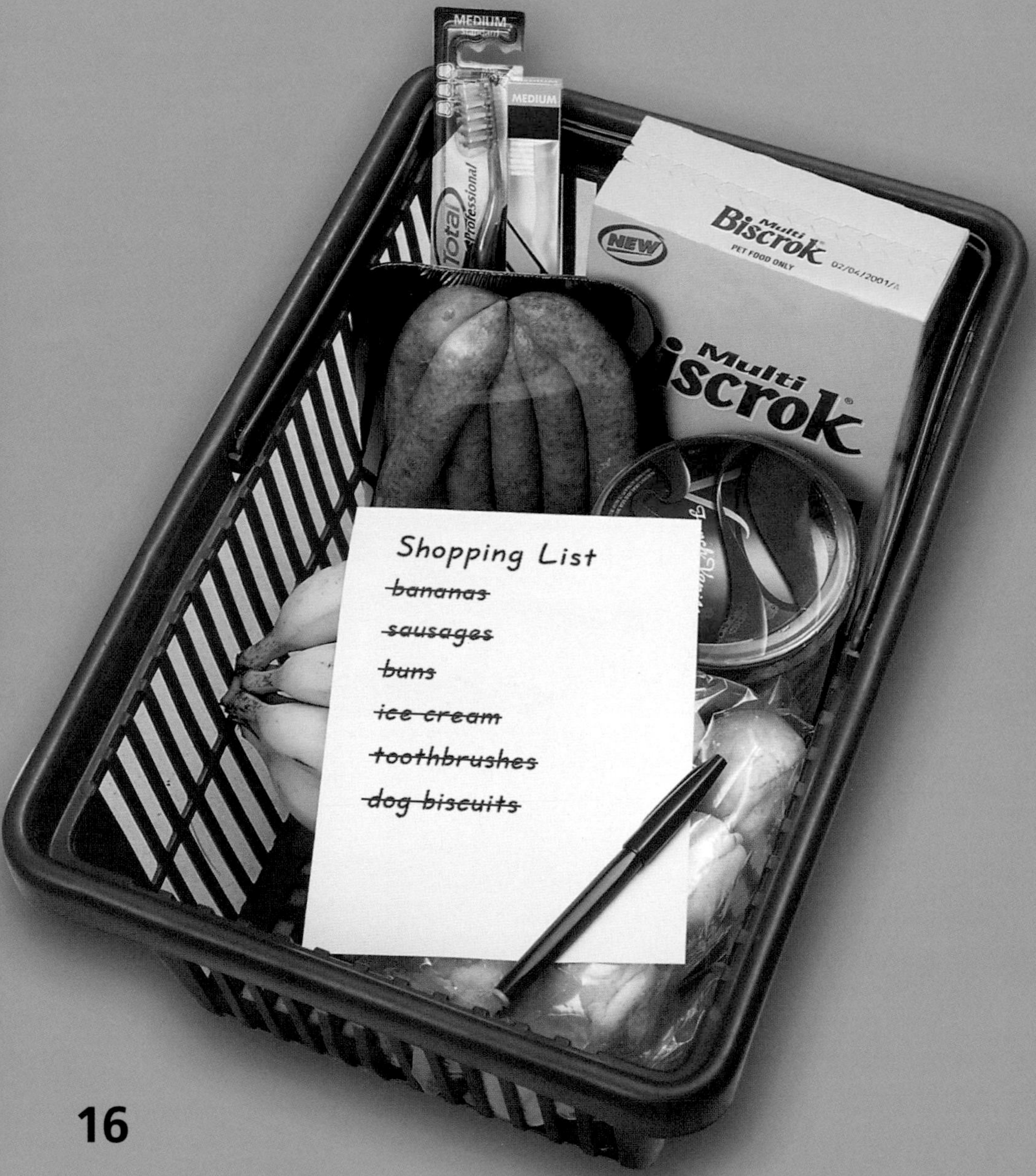
MEDIUM
MEDIUM
Total Professional
NEW
Multi Biscrok
PET FOOD ONLY
Multi Biscrok
Shopping List
~~bananas~~
~~sausages~~
~~buns~~
~~ice cream~~
~~toothbrushes~~
~~dog biscuits~~